Can Cooking

Cooking Made Easy for Your Furry Family Member

Patricia Megoulas at Briar Ridge Puppies

Canine Cooking

Cooking Made Easy for Your Furry Family Member

Patricia Megoulas at Briar Ridge Puppies

outskirtspress

DENVER, COLORADO

Table of Contents

Breakfast Foods

Comet's Favorite Pupcakes

2¾ cups water
¼ cup applesauce
2 tablespoons honey
1 egg
⅛ teaspoon vanilla
4 cups whole wheat flour
1 cup dried apple pieces
1 tablespoon baking powder
Cinnamon for sprinkling

Preheat the oven to 350 degrees.

In a small bowl, mix together water, applesauce, honey, egg, and vanilla.

In a large bowl, combine flour, the apple pieces, and baking powder. Add liquid ingredients to dry ingredients and mix until very well blended.

Pour into greased muffin pans, and then sprinkle with cinnamon. Bake 1¼ hours or until a toothpick inserted in the center comes out dry. Store in an airtight container at room temperature.

Yields 12 to 14 pupcakes.

BARF Diet Breakfast

¼ cup uncooked, rolled oats

½ cup plain yogurt

¼ cup vegetables (carrots, celery, spinach, yams, broccoli, or apples)
   lightly steamed or puréed

200 mgs vitamin C (<u>for dogs NOT humans</u>), crushed

1 teaspoon honey

1 teaspoon apple cider vinegar

1 teaspoon kelp seaweed powder

1 teaspoon alfalfa powder

1 digestive enzyme (<u>for dogs NOT humans</u>), optional

1 teaspoon flaxseed oil

¼ cup dry dog food, optional

Soak rolled oats in yogurt overnight. Mix all ingredients together and serve. Store in Refrigerator.

Puppy Quiche

4 eggs
1 tablespoon cream
⅔ cup milk
3 ounces meat, finely chopped (any type of meat), precooked
2 ounces cheddar cheese, or other type, shredded
1 whole pie crust (9 inch)
½ teaspoon garlic powder, optional

Preheat the oven to 375 degrees.

Wisk egg, cream, and milk together, then pour into pie crust. Add meat and cheese evenly distributed.

Bake 30–45 minutes or until a knife comes out clean. Store in refrigerator.

Dinner Foods

BARF Diet Dinner

¾ pound raw meat, *see Note
1 egg, raw
½ clove garlic, chopped
2 tablespoons yogurt
1 teaspoon honey
1 tablespoon apple cider vinegar
½ teaspoon flaxseed oil
1 teaspoon kelp seaweed powder
1 teaspoon alfalfa powder
250 mgs vitamin C (for dogs)
¼ cup dog food, optional

Mix all ingredients together and serve. Store in refrigerator.

*Note: raw beef chunks (not ground), raw chicken, mackerel, or lamb, etc. Twice a week use liver or kidney.

Potatoes Au Doggies

3 cups boiled potatoes, sliced
2 tablespoons vegetables, grated
½ cup cottage cheese, creamed
1 tablespoon nutritional yeast, optional
2 tablespoons carrots, grated
¼ cup whole milk
¼ cup cheddar cheese, grated

Preheat the oven to 350 degrees.

Layer in a casserole dish the first 5 ingredients. Then pour the milk on top of all; sprinkle with cheese.

Bake 15 minutes until the cheese melts and slightly browns. Serve cool. Store in refrigerator.

Sushi for Dogs

1 can salmon, pink (reserve liquid)
1 cup uncooked, brown rice
2 cups water, plus salmon liquid
1 egg, hard-boiled, chopped
½ cup peas, frozen
½ cup carrots, frozen
1 tablespoon fresh parsley, chopped
2 tablespoons cod liver oil
1 package dried seaweed sheets

Drain salmon; reserve liquid for rice. Do not remove bones or skin. Flake with a fork. Defrost peas and carrots.

In a saucepan, add salmon liquid, water, brown rice, and cook. Then set aside to cool.

In a mixing bowl, add salmon, brown rice, chopped egg, peas and carrots, parsley, and cod liver oil. Mix well.

Place a dried seaweed sheet on a flat surface and spread the mixture one-fourth inch over the sheet, leaving a one-fourth inch edge and dampen the edge with water, and then roll.

Repeat till all sheets are used or the mixture is gone.

Cut rolls into the right size for your doggie. Individually wrap in plastic wrap, then refrigerate till ready to serve.

Chewy Cheesy Pizza

CRUST:

2 cups cake flour
1¼ cups whole wheat flour
¼ cup olive oil
1 egg
1 cup water
1 teaspoon baking soda

SAUCE & TOPPINGS:

1 tomato
1 cup tomato purée
1 clove garlic
¼ cup Parmesan cheese, grated
½ teaspoon oregano
½ teaspoon basil
⅔ cup cooked rice

Preheat the oven to 325 degrees.

CRUST: Mix all ingredients together. Knead on a lightly floured surface. Spray a regular-sized, 12 inch pizza pan with nonstick spray. Next, spread the dough to the edges of the pan, forming a lip around the ends. Set aside.

SAUCE & TOPPINGS: In a food processor, blend the tomato, tomato purée, and garlic. Spoon the mixture over the pizza crust. Sprinkle the cheese and spices evenly over the sauce. Cut the pizza into slices with a pizza cutter or sharp knife.

Bake for 25 minutes. Remove from the oven and sprinkle rice evenly over the pizza. Return to the oven and bake 25 minutes more.

Chicken Chow Chow

2 chicken thighs
1 stalk celery, sliced
3 carrots, peeled and halved
2 small potatoes, peeled and cubed
2 cups rice, uncooked
Pinch of salt

Place chicken pieces in a large pot. Cover with cold water (5–6 cups). Add carrots, celery, and potatoes to the water. Add salt to taste.

Cover and simmer on low heat about 2 hours until the chicken becomes tender.

Add the rice, then cover and cook over a low heat for about 30 minutes until the rice is tender and most of the liquid is absorbed. Remove soup from the heat. Pull the chicken meat off the bone, and discard all bones.

Return shredded pieces of meat to the pot. Stir well. Cool. Store in the refrigerator or freeze.

Doggie Din Din

½ pound ground beef, turkey, chicken, or lamb
¼ cup brown rice, cooked
1 small potato
¼ cup green beans (about 5–8 beans)
¼ teaspoon garlic powder

Brown the meat in a pan. When completely cooked, drain the fat. Add the cooked rice; mix well. Set aside.

Cut the potato and beans into small, bite-sized pieces. Place in a pot with water; bring to a boil. Simmer until veggies are tender (15–20 minutes). Drain. Add the vegetables to the meat mixture. Add garlic powder and mix thoroughly on a low heat. Remove and cool. Store in refrigerator.

Doggie Stew

4 small parsnips
2 whole yellow squash, cubed
2 whole sweet potatoes, peeled and cubed
2 whole zucchini, cubed
5 whole tomatoes, canned
1 15 ounce can garbanzo beans or chickpeas
½ cup couscous
1 teaspoon coriander, ground
½ teaspoon turmeric, ground
½ teaspoon cinnamon, ground
½ teaspoon ginger, ground
¼ teaspoon cumin, ground
3 cups water or chicken stock

Combine all the ingredients in a large saucepan. Bring to a boil, lower the heat, and simmer until the vegetables are tender, about 30 minutes.

Place over cooked brown rice and serve. Store in refrigerator.

Burritos

1 tablespoon oil
12 ounces cooked beef or chicken, cut into ½ inch strips
1 clove garlic, minced
3 tablespoons chunky peanut butter
1 23 ounce can sweet potatoes, drained
1 15 ounce can black beans, rinsed
1 teaspoon chili powder
1 teaspoon cumin
½ teaspoon cinnamon
2 teaspoons beef bouillon, powder
6 flour tortillas (10 inch)
2 tablespoons cilantro, chopped
6 tablespoons cheddar cheese, shredded
6 tablespoons veggies, shredded (carrots, green beans, broccoli, etc.)

Heat oil in a large skillet, over medium heat until hot. Add garlic; cook and stir 2–3 minutes or until tender. Stir in peanut butter, sweet potatoes, and beans; mash slightly. Add cumin, cinnamon, chili powder, and beef bouillon; mix well.

Reduce heat to low. Add beef, cover, and simmer 2–3 minutes or until thoroughly heated, stirring occasionally.

Meanwhile, heat tortillas, according to package directions.

To serve: Spoon and spread one-half cup of the mixture across the center third of each tortilla with one piece of meat in the center. Top each with 1 tablespoon sour cream, 1 teaspoon cilantro, 1 tablespoon of shredded cheese to cover the mixture. Fold the sides of each tortilla 1 inch over the filling. Fold bottom third of the tortilla over the filling. Roll again to enclose the filling.

Store in refrigerator.

Stew Chowder

1 tablespoon olive oil
2 pounds beef, chicken, lamb, fish, or liver
2 cups cabbage, chopped
3 cloves garlic, minced
1 18 ounce can sweet potatoes, drained and chopped
1 14½ ounce can tomatoes (do not drain)
1½ cups tomato juice
¾ cup apple juice
1 teaspoon ginger root, grated
2 cups cut green beans, frozen
⅓ cup peanut butter
6 cups brown rice, cooked

Heat oil in a large skillet, over medium-high heat. Cook the beef, then add the cabbage and garlic. Cook, stirring until the cabbage is tender-crisp, about 5 minutes. Stir in the sweet potatoes, tomatoes, tomato juice, apple juice, and ginger. Reduce the heat to medium-low; cover. Simmer until hot and bubbling, about 6 minutes.

Stir in the green beans and simmer, uncovered, for 5 minutes. Stir in the peanut butter until well-blended and hot, about 1 minute.

Spoon over cooked brown rice. Store in refrigerator.

Doggie Loaf

2⅛ cups water
2 cups brown rice
2 large potatoes
2 large carrots
1⅛ pounds pumpkin (not pie filling)
2 cloves garlic
¾ bunch silver beet
1 cup whole meal pasta or soya pasta
2 cups rolled oats
1 cup whole meal flour
1⅛ pounds liver or fish, minced
3 eggs

Preheat oven to 350 degrees.

Boil the rice in water for 10–15 minutes and chop the veggies and add to rice with the pasta. Cook for 10 minutes. Turn off the heat and leave to cool.

Add minced meat, eggs, herbs, rolled oats, and flour. Mix together. Add more oats or flour if the mixture is sticky. (It should be like a fruit cake mix.) Spoon into oiled and floured loaf tins.

Bake for 1 hour.

Remove from the tins, turn the oven off, and return the loaves to the oven 5–10 minutes to firm the bottom crust.

Remove from the oven, cool, then use immediately or wrap and freeze.

Makes 3 to 4 loaves. Store in refrigerator.

Favorite Cheese Nuggets

1 cup oatmeal, uncooked
1½ cups hot water
4 ounces cheddar cheese, grated
1 egg, beaten
1 cup wheat germ
¼ cup margarine
½ cup powdered milk
¼ teaspoon salt
1 cup cornmeal
3 cups whole wheat flour

Preheat the oven to 300 degrees.

In a large bowl, pour hot water over the oatmeal and margarine. Let stand for 5 minutes. Stir in powdered milk, grated cheese, salt, and egg. Add cornmeal and wheat germ. Mix well.

Add flour, one-third cup at a time, mixing well after each addition. Knead 3–4 minutes, adding more flour if necessary to make a very stiff dough.

Roll dough to a one-half inch thickness. Cut into bone-shaped biscuits and place on a greased baking sheet.

Bake for 1 hour. Turn off the heat and leave in the oven for 2–3 hours.

Yields approximately 2¼ pounds of nuggets. Store in airtight container in room temperature.

Doggie Goulash

1 pound ground beef, ground turkey, or ground venison

2 cups cooked, brown rice

3 cups vegetables, cut (broccoli, asparagus, sweet potatoes, green beans, carrots, spinach, kale)

2 eggs with shells

1 can mackerel

2 cloves garlic, minced

1 pound chicken liver or gizzards

Pulverize veggies, either in a blender or processor. Mix all ingredients together in a big pot. Add enough water to cover and simmer for about 2 hours, stirring occasionally.

Cool and place into containers, enough for one feeding in each container, and freeze.

Thaw in the fridge

Serve with one-half cup of dry dog food.

Green Bean Grubs

1 pound green beans, sliced, fresh or frozen
1 can cream of chicken soup
½ cup milk
½ cup cheddar cheese, plus extra for topping

Preheat the oven to 350 degrees.

Mix all ingredients together except beans. Place beans in an oven casserole, add the sauce mixture, and stir well.

Cover and bake for 25 minutes.

Uncover the casserole and sprinkle the top with more cheddar cheese. Bake 5 minutes more. Remove and cool.

Lamb Dinner

1 pound lamb, ground, cooked
4 cups cooked brown rice
1 cup yogurt
2 cloves garlic, crushed
¼ cup green beans, chopped, frozen
¼ cup carrots, chopped, frozen
¼ cup kale, chopped, frozen

Defrost frozen veggies and chop to the desired size.

In a large bowl, mix cooked lamb, cooked rice, chopped vegetables, garlic, and yogurt. Slightly heat if desired to serve.

Refrigerate or freeze portions.

Yields 3 to 6 servings.

Meat and Grain Menu

2 cups brown rice, cooked
⅔ cup cooked meat (beef, chicken, lamb, or liver)
2 teaspoons vegetable oil
¼ cup vegetables (broccoli, carrots, beets, peas)

Mix the above. Serve slightly warm.

Meatballs

2 cups uncooked, rolled oats
2 eggs
2 pounds ground turkey, cooked
½ cup grated Parmesan cheese
1 teaspoon oregano
½ teaspoon garlic powder

Preheat the oven to 350 degrees.

Mix all of the ingredients together in a large bowl and stir well.

Scoop a tablespoon of the mixture and roll it into a ball with your hands. Then continue making more meatballs with the rest of the mixture. Put the meatballs in an ungreased baking pan and bake them for approximately 30 minutes. Allow them to cool to normal temperature before serving them.

Keep them in a covered container in the refrigerator for up to 3 days or wrap and store them in the freezer for up to 2 months.

Yields approximately 24 doggie meatballs.

Meatball Mania

½ pound ground beef
2 tablespoons cheddar or mozzarella cheese, grated
1 carrot, finely grated
½ teaspoon garlic powder
½ cup bread crumbs
1 egg, beaten
½ tablespoon tomato paste

Preheat the oven to 350 degrees.

Combine all ingredients together; mix thoroughly. Roll into meatballs and place on a cookie sheet sprayed with nonstick cooking spray.

Bake 15–20 minutes or until they are brown and firm. Cool and store in the fridge or freezer.

Mutten Loaf

½ cup barley
4 cups chicken broth
1½ pounds ground chicken or turkey
½ cup cottage cheese
2 eggs
½ cup rolled oats
¼ cup carrots, finely chopped
¼ cup spinach, finely chopped
¼ cup zucchini, finely chopped
2 cloves garlic
1 tablespoon olive oil

Preheat the oven to 350 degrees.

Add barley and chicken broth to a saucepan and bring to a boil, reduce heat, then simmer for 50 minutes. Set aside and let cool.

In a large mixing bowl, add meat, cottage cheese, veggies, and eggs. Mix thoroughly. Add wheat germ, cooled mixture, and olive oil. Mix well.

Pour into a loaf pan and bake 1 hour or until done.

Fiona's Rice and Hamburger

2 cups uncooked, brown rice
½ pound ground beef
1 teaspoon vegetable oil
1 clove garlic
½ cup carrots, broccoli, or spinach
4 cups water

Put all ingredients into a large pot, boil until cooked, then cool and serve.

Mutt Balls

1 cup natural dry dog food
2 eggs, beaten lightly
1 teaspoon cod liver oil
⅓ cup cold water
2 dashes garlic powder
½ cup cream of chicken soup, condensed

Grind dry dog food until smooth in a food processor or blender. Lightly beat eggs and add oil. Mix all moist ingredients together except the soup. Add to the dry ingredients. Form into one-half inch balls.

In a large pan, bring 1 quart of water to a boil. Add one-half cup of chicken soup. Drop the balls into the boiling water. Boil for 3 minutes. Remove the balls from the water, drain, and cool. Refrigerate.

Poodle Pasta

3½ cups whole wheat flour
8 ounces beef liver
3 eggs
1 tablespoon olive oil
8 tablespoons butter, optional

Purée beef liver in a blender until smooth. Add eggs and blend for about a minute.

Put flour in a large mixing bowl and make a well in the center of the flour. Pour liver and egg mixture into the well, along with olive oil. Mix well until thoroughly combined.

Turn the dough out on a floured board and knead well for at least 5 minutes or until smooth and shiny.

Wrap the dough in plastic wrap and let it rest in the refrigerator for at least 1 hour, but no longer than 2 days.

When ready to make pasta, divide the dough into 8 equal portions, approximately 4 ounces each. Form into desired pasta shapes with hands or use a pasta machine.

Cook in rapidly boiling water until al dente. For thin noodles, approximately 10 minutes; for thicker noodles, a few minutes longer.

Drain noodles and toss with 1 tablespoon of butter per serving.

Yields 2 pounds.

SERVING IDEAS: Toss cooked pasta with finely shredded fresh vegetables such as carrots, zucchini, broccoli, or sweet potatoes before serving.

Mix cooked pasta with 2 tablespoons of low-fat cottage cheese and/or yogurt per serving for a smooth, creamy sauce.

Poodle Training Meatballs

  10 pounds ground beef
  1 lg. box Total cereal
  1 lg. box oatmeal
  1 jar wheat germ
  1¼ cups vegetable oil
  1¼ cups molasses
  10 raw eggs
  10 envelopes of unflavored gelatin
  1 pinch salt

Mix all ingredients together into a 1-inch meatball-size serving. Divide into 10 quart freezer bags and freeze.

Thaw as needed.

To put on weight, use 2–3 meatballs a day, plus regular food. As treats for dogs without weight problems, divide a ball into quarters.

Trail Doggie Grub

2 cups barley, cooked
1 cup lentils, cooked
1 cup vegetables (carrot, kale, sweet potato, asparagus, zucchini)
2 tablespoons cod liver oil
1 pound meat (beef, lamb, etc.)
1 cup beef broth

Cut meat to bite-size portions. Place in a saucepan, along with beef broth, vegetables, and cod liver oil.

Cook 10 minutes. Add water if more moisture is needed during cooking time.

Add cooked barley and cooked lentils. Mix well. Allow to cool and serve.

Veggie Vittles

1 egg, beaten
⅓ cup applesauce
1 cup vegetables, mashed or grated (zucchini, peas, carrots, potatoes)
1 cup cooked brown rice
1 tablespoon brewer's yeast

Preheat the oven to 350 degrees.

Mix all ingredients well. Drop by rounded teaspoonful onto a greased cookie sheet.

Bake for 12 minutes or until lightly browned and firm.

Cool. Store in the fridge or freeze.

Canine's Variety Stew

2 cups barley
½ cup wild rice
9 cups chicken broth
4 cups rabbit, boned, *see Note
½ cup kale, chopped fine, **see Note
½ cup asparagus, chopped fine
½ cup lima beans, chopped fine
½ cup carrots, chopped fine
1 cup potatoes, chopped fine
3 cloves garlic, chopped fine
⅓ cup canola oil
1 cup yogurt

In a large pot, place the bones of rabbits and the chicken broth. Bring to a rapid boil. Add the long-cooking wild rice and barley. Reduce heat to a simmer and cover.

After 20 minutes add the rabbit meat and cook another 30 minutes.

Chop the vegetables, place in a mixing bowl, and add canola oil and yogurt. Mix well.

Allow barley and wild rice to cool. Remove all bones. Drain the liquid if needed.

Pour into the mixing bowl and mix all ingredients well.

Refrigerate or freeze leftovers in separate containers.

*Note: Two rabbits, 4 to 6 pounds each. Bone the rabbits and cube to the proper size for your dog. Add the bones to the chicken broth.

**Note: Frozen vegetables may be used; run under cold water to defrost.

Walleye for Dogs

3 pounds walleye pike fillets
2 ounces chicken livers, diced fine
2 cups fish stock
3 cups cooked brown rice
¼ cup cooked wild rice
¼ cup kale, frozen
½ cup green beans, frozen
¼ cup collard greens, frozen
¼ cup corn, frozen
¼ cup potatoes, frozen
1 tablespoon cod liver oil

Preheat the oven to 350 degrees.

In a baking dish, add walleye fillets and diced chicken livers. Pour in fish stock and cod liver oil. Add frozen veggies, cover, and bake 20–30 minutes or till done.

In a large bowl, add cooked rice and the juices from the baking dish, along with the cooked veggies. Mix well.

Chunk the walleye into a size for your dog and mix well. If needed, chop vegetables to the right size for your dog.

Cool and serve. Freeze leftovers or keep in the fridge covered.

Breads and Muffins

Parker's Bagels

1 cup whole wheat flour
1 cup unbleached all-purpose flour
1 package yeast (¼ ounce)
1 cup chicken broth, warmed
1 tablespoon honey

Preheat the oven to 375 degrees.

In a large bowl, combine the whole wheat flour with the yeast. Add two-thirds cup of chicken broth and honey. Beat for about 3 minutes. Gradually add the remaining flour.

Knead the dough for a few minutes until smooth and moist, but not wet (use reserved broth as necessary).

Cover the dough and let it rest for about 5 minutes. Divide the dough into about 15 to 20 pieces, rolling each piece into a smooth ball.

Punch a hole into each ball with your finger or end of a spoon and gently pull the dough so the hole is about one-half inch wide. Don't be too fussy here. The little bagels rise into shape when they bake.

Place all the bagels on a greased cookie sheet and allow to rise for 5 minutes. Bake for 25 minutes. Turn the heat off and allow the bagels to cool in the oven.

Cheesy Carrot Muffins

1 cup all-purpose flour
1 cup whole wheat flour
1 tablespoon baking powder
1 cup cheddar cheese, shredded
1 cup carrots, grated
2 large eggs
1 cup milk

Preheat the oven to 350 degrees.

Grease a muffin tin or line it with paper baking cups. Combine the flours and baking powder and mix well. Add the cheese and carrots and use your fingers to mix them into the flour until they are well distributed.

In another bowl, beat the eggs. Then whisk in the milk and vegetable oil. Pour this over the flour mixture and stir gently until just combined. Fill the muffin cups three-quarters full with the mixture. Bake 20–25 minutes or until the muffins feel springy. Be sure to let the muffins cool before letting your dog do any taste testing! One muffin for a medium-large dog, half a muffin for a toy or small dog.

Corgi Crumpets

2½ cups cornmeal
1½ cups cake flour
2 tablespoons vegetable oil
1 egg
⅔ cup honey
½ teaspoon baking powder
½ teaspoon cinnamon
½ teaspoon nutmeg
1 small apple
1⅓ cups water
½ cup rolled oats

Preheat the oven to 350 degrees.

In a bowl, mix all ingredients except the apple and rolled oats. Grate apple into the mixture. With an ice-cream scoop, fill into muffin pans lined with paper baking cups and sprinkle with oats. Bake 40 minutes.

Hors D'ogs

¼ cup cheddar cheese, grated
2 tablespoons safflower oil
½ cup Rice Krispies
½ teaspoon garlic, minced
¼ cup Swiss cheese, grated

Combine cheeses, garlic, and oil. Using plastic wrap, shape the mixture into a log about 1 inch in diameter and 8 inches long. Roll the log in Rice Krispies. Refrigerate. Slice into half inch squares and serve.

Massive Munchy Muffins

2 carrots
2¾ cups water
1 egg
¼ teaspoon vanilla extract
2 tablespoons honey
1½ banana, *see Note
4 cups whole wheat flour
1 tablespoon baking powder
1 tablespoon cinnamon
1 tablespoon nutmeg

Preheat the oven to 350 degrees.

Shred the carrot with a hand shredder or in a blender. Mix all wet ingredients together in a bowl, then add the puréed banana. Mix together thoroughly. Set aside.

Combine the dry ingredients. Add the wet ingredients to the dry ingredients and mix thoroughly, leaving no dry mixture on the bottom.

Coat a 12 muffin pan with nonstick spray. Fill each muffin space three-fourths full. Bake 1 hour.

NOTE: The banana should be overripe. Replace the banana with one apple for a different flavor!

Scrumptious Carob Bake

6 cups white rice flour
⅛ cup peanut oil
⅛ cup margarine (safflower oil type)
1 tablespoon brown sugar
4 ounces carob chips, melted
1 cup water
¼ cup molasses
½ cup powdered milk

Preheat the oven to 300 degrees.

Mix dry ingredients in a large bowl. Add remaining ingredients and mix until blended. Dough will be stiff. Chill.

Roll dough on a greased cookie pan and cut into shapes ½ inch thick. Bake for 1 hour.

Sheltie Scones

2½ cups self-rising flour
1 cup beef liver, chopped
½ cup water or beef stock
½ cup milk
2 tablespoons butter
¼ teaspoon salt

CHOPPED LIVER: Boil the liver until it is gray with the consistency of rubber. Or if you have a microwave, cook it on high for about 8 minutes. Chop it up into small pieces. Cool. Place the pieces into airtight bags and refrigerate. Use liver pieces as treats when training.

SCONES: Sift flour and salt into a bowl. Rub in butter. Add chopped liver. Use a knife to stir in milk and enough water to mix into a sticky dough.

Turn dough onto a lightly floured surface, then knead quickly and lightly until the dough is smooth.

Press dough out evenly to about 2 inches and cut into rounds. Place on a greased tray and bake in a very hot oven (400* F) for 15 minutes.

Yields 16 to 18.

Biscuits

A Cheesy Dog Biscuit

1½ cups whole wheat flour
1¼ cups cheddar cheese, grated
¼ pound margarine (corn oil), room temperature
1 clove garlic, crushed
1 pinch salt
¼ cup milk (or as needed)

Preheat the oven to 375 degrees.

Grate the cheese into a bowl and let stand until it reaches room temperature. Cream the cheese with the softened margarine, garlic, salt, and flour. Add enough milk to form into a ball.

Chill for half an hour.

Roll the mixture onto a floured board. Cut into shapes and bake 15 minutes or until slightly brown and firm.

Yields 2 to 3 dozen, depending on size.

Comet's Dog Biscuits

2½ cups whole wheat flour
½ cup nonfat powdered milk
½ teaspoon salt
½ teaspoon garlic powder
1 teaspoon brown sugar
6 tablespoons beef fat
1 egg, beaten
½ cup ice water

Preheat the oven to 350 degrees.

Lightly oil a cookie sheet. Combine flour, dry milk, salt, garlic powder, and sugar. Cut in meat drippings until the mixture resembles cornmeal. Mix in the egg. Add enough water so that the mixture forms a ball.

Using your fingers, pat out dough onto the cookie sheet to ½ inch thick. Cut with a cookie cutter or knife and remove scraps. Scraps can be formed again.

Bake 25 to 30 minutes. Remove from the tray and cool on a rack.

Apple Cinnamon Doggie Biscuits

1 package apples, dried
1 teaspoon cinnamon (I usually just shake some in)
1 tablespoon parsley, freeze-dried
1 tablespoon garlic powder
1 cup ice water
½ cup corn oil
5 cups all-purpose flour
½ cup nonfat powdered milk
2 large eggs
1 tablespoon corn oil

Preheat the oven to 350 degrees.

Put the apples in a food processor so that pieces are small. Combine all of the ingredients in a bowl. Add oil or water if the dough is too dry.

Using a rolling pin, roll out the dough to about 3/16 inches thick (you can roll it thinner or thicker). Then cut into shapes with a cookie cutter and place them on greased, cookie sheets. Bake 20–25 minutes (until golden brown).

NOTE: if you substitute cornmeal for the flour, just subtract about ¾ cup from the flour for the correct amount of cornmeal.

Candy Girl's Dog Biscuits

2½ cups whole wheat flour
½ cup nonfat dry milk powder
1 teaspoon garlic powder
1 egg, beaten
Meat drippings, broth, or water from canned tuna (for flavor)

Preheat the oven to 350 degrees.

Combine flour, powdered milk, and garlic powder in a medium-sized bowl. Add beaten egg and liquid for flavoring, and mix well with your hands. The dough should be very stiff. If necessary add more flavoring liquid.

On a floured surface, roll out the dough to one-fourth inch thick. Cut with shaped cookie cutters of your choice.

Place biscuits on greased, cookie sheets and bake 30 minutes.

Biscuits

1 cup oatmeal, uncooked
⅓ cup margarine
1 tablespoon beef bouillon granules
5½ cups hot water
1 tablespoon garlic powder, optional
¾ cup nonfat powdered milk
¾ cup cornmeal
3 cups whole wheat flour
1 egg, beaten

Preheat the oven to 325 degrees.

Pour hot water over oatmeal, margarine, and bouillon; let stand for 6 minutes.

Stir in milk, cornmeal, and egg. Add flour, half a cup at a time; mix well after each addition.

Knead 3–4 minutes, adding more flour if necessary to make a very STIFF dough.

Roll or pat dough to half an inch thickness. Cut into dog bone shapes with a cookie cutter.

Bake 50 minutes on a baking greased, cookie sheet. Cool, then store in an airtight container in room temperature.

Thaleia's Bones

2¼ teaspoons dry yeast
¼ cup warm water (liquid measure)
1 teaspoon sugar
3½ cups all-purpose flour
2 cups whole wheat flour
2 cups cracked wheat
1 cup rye flour
½ cup nonfat powdered milk
4 teaspoons kelp powder
4 cups beef broth or chicken

GLAZE:

1 large egg
2 tablespoons milk

Preheat the oven to 300 degrees.

Sprinkle the dry yeast or crumple the compressed yeast over the water (110 degrees if you use dry yeast; 100 degrees if compressed yeast). Add sugar and allow the yeast to sit in a draft-free spot for 10 to 20 minutes. The mixture should be full of bubbles.

In a large bowl, place all the dry ingredients and stir to blend them. Add the yeast mixture and 3 cups of the broth. Using your hands, in the bowl, mix to form the dough, adding more broth if needed to make the dough smooth and supple. Divide the batch in half and work with half of a batch at a time.

Knead the dough briefly on a lightly floured counter. (Keep the second batch of dough covered with a moist towel while shaping and cutting the first mixture.)

Roll out the dough with a rolling pin into an 18 x 13 x ¼ inch rectangle. Cut it into desired shapes, using a 3–3½ inch bone cutter or a 2½ inch round cookie cutter. Reroll the scraps. Repeat the procedure with the remaining dough. Place on cookie sheets lined with parchment or aluminum foil.

GLAZE: For an attractive shine, lightly beat together the egg and milk. Brush the glaze on the cookies. Bake for 45–60 minutes or until brown and firm.

For even baking, rotate the cookie sheets from the top to the bottom three-quarters of the way through the baking period.

Use a small, angled metal spatula or pancake turner to transfer the cookies to wire racks to cool completely.

Store in an airtight container at room temperature. The dough must be used immediately. The baked cookies will keep for many months.

Allow the cookie sheets to cool completely between batches.

Bones

½ pound ground beef, uncooked
¼ cup chicken broth
⅓ cup black beans, cooked, mashed
⅓ cup cottage cheese
1 teaspoon soy sauce

Preheat the oven to 375 degrees.

Combine ground meat and chicken broth in a bowl. Add the black beans and cottage cheese. Add soy sauce. Mix all of the ingredients together thoroughly.

Mold the mixture into bone shapes and place on a cookie sheet. Bake 45 minutes. Cool.

Hobo's Biscuits

3½ cups whole wheat flour
2 cups Quaker oats
1 cup milk
½ cup hot water
2 beef or chicken bouillon cubes
½ cup meat drippings

Preheat the oven to 300 degrees.

Dissolve bouillon cubes in hot water. Add milk and drippings and beat.

In a separate bowl, mix flour and oatmeal. Pour liquid ingredients into dry ingredients and mix well. Press onto an ungreased cookie sheet and cut into shapes desired.

Bake 1 hour.

Turn off the heat and leave in the oven to harden. Refrigerate after baking.

Bow-Wow Biscuits

2½ cups whole wheat flour
½ cup wheat germ
½ cup nonfat powdered milk
½ teaspoon salt
½ teaspoon garlic powder
8 tablespoons bacon grease or margarine
1 egg, beaten
1 teaspoon brown sugar
2 tablespoons beef broth or chicken
½ cup ice water
6 slices bacon, crumbled, optional
½ cup cheddar cheese, shredded, optional

Preheat the oven to 350 degrees.

In a big mixing bowl, mix all the ingredients thoroughly. Roll the dough with a rolling pin and cut with a cookie cutter. Place on a greased, cookie tray.

Bake 20–25 minutes.

Bread Machine Dog Biscuits

¾ cup beef stock, *see Note
1 egg
3 tablespoons oil
1 cup all-purpose flour
1 cup whole wheat flour
⅓ cup bulgur, **see Note
⅓ cup bran
¼ cup nonfat powdered milk
¼ teaspoon garlic powder
1½ teaspoons yeast
Preheat the oven to 325 degrees.

Place ingredients in a bread pan according to the manufacturer's directions and press "dough" cycle. When the machine beeps, remove the dough and place on a lightly floured countertop. Roll out with a rolling pin to one-fourth inch thickness.

Using a dog bone cookie cutter (or any small seasonal cookie cutters), cut out dog biscuits and place on a lightly greased cookie sheet or one sprinkled with cornmeal. Reroll scraps and repeat till all the dough is used up. Place in a warm location and let rise 30 minutes.

Bake 30 minutes or until brown and no longer soft. Place on a wire rack to cool. Store in an airtight container.

* Chicken, vegetable, or use hot water and 2–3 bouillon cubes.

**If you don't have bulgur, substitute with a 7-grain cereal.

Breath Busters Biscuits

1½ cups whole wheat flour
1½ cups Bisquick baking mix
½ cup mint leaves, loosely packed
¼ cup milk
4 tablespoons margarine
1 egg
1½ tablespoons maple syrup or corn syrup

Preheat the oven to 375 degrees.

Combine all ingredients in a food processor and process until well mixed and the mint is chopped and a large ball forms.

Press or roll on a nonstick surface (floured board or ceramic) to one-fourth or one-half inch thick. Cut into 1 x 2 inch strips or use a bone-shaped cookie cutter. Place on a nonstick cookie tray.

Bake 20 minutes or until lightly browned.

Cool and store in an airtight container.

Makes approximately 30 medium-sized biscuits.

Makaros's Dog Biscuits

1 cup whole wheat flour
½ cup all-purpose flour
¾ cup nonfat dry milk powder
½ cup oats, rolled (raw), quick cooking
½ cup yellow cornmeal
1 teaspoon sugar

Cut in one-third cup shortening until the mixture resembles coarse crumbs. Stir in 1 egg. Dissolve 1 tablespoon of instant chicken or beef bouillon granules in half a cup of water. Stir the liquid into the flour mixture with a fork.

Form dough into a ball and knead on a floured board for 5 minutes. Divide the ball in half and roll each portion until half an inch thick. Use a cookie cutter or shape the biscuits.

Put 6 on a plate and microwave at a medium heat for 5–10 minutes or until firm and dry to touch. Turn the biscuits over after half the cooking time and continue the cooking process.

Cheese and Bacon Dog Biscuits

¾ cup all-purpose flour
½ teaspoon baking soda
½ teaspoon salt
⅔ cup butter
⅔ cup brown sugar
1 egg
1 teaspoon vanilla extract
1½ cups uncooked, oatmeal
1 cup cheddar cheese, shredded
½ cup wheat germ
½ pound bacon or bacon bits

Preheat the oven to 350 degrees.

Combine flour, soda, and salt; mix well and set aside. Cream butter and sugar, then beat in egg and vanilla. Add flour mixture and mix well.

Stir in oats, cheese, wheat germ, and bacon.

Drop by rounded tablespoons onto ungreased baking sheets.

Bake 16 minutes.

Cool and let the critters enjoy!

Chicken Flavored Dog Biscuits

2½ teaspoons dry yeast
1 teaspoon sugar
¼ cup warm water
1 teaspoon salt, optional
1 egg
1 cup chicken broth, slightly warmed
1 cup whole wheat flour
½ cup rye flour, optional
½ cup cornmeal
1 cup cracked wheat
1½ cups all-purpose flour

Preheat the oven to 300 degrees.

In a large bowl, dissolve yeast and 1 teaspoon of sugar to warm water to active yeast. Add salt, egg, and the warmed chicken broth. Add rye and whole wheat flour and mix. Slowly add the all-purpose flour until a stiff dough is formed. Knead by hand for only a couple minutes, just enough to get the dough to hold together.

Roll out dough one-fourth inch thick and cut with cookie cutters. Place biscuits on a large greased, cookie tray.

Bake 45 minutes, and then turn off the oven. Let them sit in the oven overnight. In the morning they will be real hard and good for your dog's teeth.

You could also vary this recipe by adding milk for a milk-bone type biscuit or use shortening for a little extra fat. Try different liquids and even honey or molasses.

Dog Biscuits #1

2½ cups whole wheat flour
1 teaspoon brown sugar
½ cup nonfat powdered milk
6 tablespoons butter
½ teaspoon salt
1 egg, beaten
½ teaspoon garlic powder
½ cup ice water

Preheat the oven to 350 degrees.

Combine the flour, milk, salt, garlic powder, and sugar. Cut in butter until mixture resembles cornmeal. Mix in the egg, then add enough ice water to form a ball. Pat dough to half an inch thick on a lightly oiled cookie sheet.

Cut out shapes with a cookie cutter or biscuit cutter and bake on the cookie sheet for 25 minutes.

Remove from the oven and cool on a wire rack.

To vary the flavor and texture, at the time the egg is added, add any of the following: 1 cup puréed cooked green vegetables or carrots, 6 tablespoons of whole wheat or rye kernels, or 3 tablespoons of liver powder. (The last two items are available in health food stores.) Butter, margarine, shortening, or meat juices may be used.

Dog Biscuits #2

BISCUITS:

  1 envelope dry yeast
  1 cup rye flour
  ¼ cup warm water
  ½ cup nonfat powdered milk
  1 pinch sugar
  4 teaspoons kelp powder
  3½ cups all-purpose flour
  4 cups beef or chicken broth
  2 cups whole wheat flour
  2 cups cracked wheat or 1 cup cornmeal

GLAZE:

  1 large egg
  2 tablespoons milk
  Preheat the oven to 300 degrees.

BISCUITS: Sprinkle the dry yeast or crumble the compressed yeast over the water. Add a pinch of sugar and allow the yeast to sit in a draft-free spot 10–20 minutes. The mixture should be full of bubbles. If not, the yeast is too old to be useful. Stir well to dissolve the yeast.

In a large bowl, place all the dry ingredients and stir well to blend them. Add the yeast mixture and 3 cups of broth.

Mix the dough with your hands adding more broth if needed to make the dough smooth and supple.

Divide the dough into two halves. Knead half the batch briefly on a lightly floured counter. (Keep the second batch of dough covered with a moist towel while shaping and cutting the first batch.)

Roll out the dough into an 18 x 13 x ¼ inch rectangle. Cut into desired shapes using a 2½ inch or 3½ inch cookie cutter. Place on ungreased, cookie sheets. Reroll the scraps. Repeat the procedure with the remaining dough.

GLAZE: For an attractive shine, lightly beat together the egg and the milk. Brush the glaze on the cookies. Bake 45–60 minutes, or until brown and firm.

Rotate the cookie sheets from top to bottom three-fourths of the way through the baking period. Use a small, angled metal spatula to transfer the cookies to wire racks to cool completely.

Dog Biscuits #3

3½ cups all-purpose flour
4 teaspoons salt
2 cups whole wheat flour
½ cup nonfat powdered milk
1 cup rye flour
1 egg
1 cup cornmeal
1 package dry yeast (1 tablespoon)
1 teaspoon sugar
2 cups cracked wheat
1 pint chicken stock

Preheat the oven to 300 degrees.

Dissolve the yeast and sugar in ¼ cup of warm water, let bubble. Add chicken stock and pour into dry ingredients. Knead for 3 minutes, working into a stiff dough.

Roll the dough into a one-fourth inch thick sheet and cut with cookie cutters (cutters shaped like dog biscuits are available) place on ungreased, cookie sheet.

Bake 45 minutes, then turn the oven off and leave biscuits in the oven overnight. In the morning, the biscuits will be bone hard.

NOTE: This dough is extremely stiff to work with, but the end product is excellent!

Dog Biscuits #4

2¾ cups whole wheat flour
½ cup nonfat powdered milk
1 teaspoon salt
¼ teaspoon garlic powder
1 egg
6 tablespoons vegetable oil
8–10 tablespoons water
2 jars meat baby food (beef, chicken, or lamb), strained

Preheat the oven to 350 degrees.

Mix all ingredients together and knead 3 minutes. Roll out to ¼ inch thick. Use a dog bone-shaped cookie cutter and place shaped biscuits on an ungreased baking sheet.

Bake 20–25 minutes.

Yields 2 dozen doggie biscuits.

Dog Biscuits #5

1 cup whole wheat flour
1 cup white flour
½ cup non-fat powdered milk
½ cup wheat germ
½ teaspoon salt
6 tablespoons shortening
1 egg, slightly beaten
1 teaspoon brown sugar
½ cup cold water

Preheat the oven to 325 degrees.

Stir dry ingredients, and then cut in the shortening. Stir egg and brown sugar into the flour mixture. Blend in water. Knead dough 10–12 strokes. Flour the surface if the dough sticks. Roll dough out to approximately three-eighth inches.

Cut with a bone-shaped cookie cutter.

Bake 30 minutes or until the dough is firm to the touch.

Yields approximately 40 biscuits.

Dog Biscuits for Your Favorite Dog

2 cups whole wheat flour
1 cup cornmeal
⅔ cup brewer's yeast
2 teaspoons garlic powder
½ teaspoon salt
2 egg yolks
3 beef or chicken bouillon cubes
½ cup boiling water

Preheat the oven to 375 degrees.

Mix all ingredients well. Divide the dough in half and work with half the dough at a time, keep rest of dough covered. Roll dough to 3/8 inch thickness. Cut into desired shapes.

Bake 20 minutes on an ungreased cookie sheet. Turn the oven off but leave the biscuits in the oven until they are crunchy.

Yields approximately 1 pound of dog biscuits

Dog Bones

2¼ cups whole wheat flour
½ cup nonfat powdered milk
1 egg
½ cup vegetable oil
1 beef bouillon cube
½ cup hot water
1 tablespoon brown sugar

Preheat the oven to 300 degrees.

In a large mixing bowl, combine all ingredients, stirring until well blended. Knead dough 2 minutes.

On a floured surface, use a floured rolling pin to roll out dough to one-fourth inch thickness. Using a bone-shaped cookie cutter, cut into bones.

Bake 30 minutes on an ungreased cookie sheet. Remove from the pan and cool on a wire rack.

Doggie Biscuits

¾ cup hot water or meat juice
⅓ cup margarine
½ cup nonfat powdered milk
½ teaspoon salt
1 egg, beaten
3 cups whole wheat flour

Preheat the oven to 325 degrees.

Mix all ingredients well. Roll into small logs in your hands and bake 50 minutes. Let cool and cut into 1 inch pieces. Store in airtight container, at room temperature.

Doggie Bone Treats

1 cup all-purpose flour
1 cup whole wheat flour
½ cup wheat germ
½ cup nonfat powdered milk
3 tablespoons vegetable shortening
1 teaspoon brown sugar
½ teaspoon salt
1 egg
⅓ cup water

Preheat the oven to 350 degrees.

Coat a cookie sheet with nonstick cooking spray. In a large bowl, combine both flours, wheat germ, nonfat powdered milk, shortening, brown sugar, and salt. Mix until crumbly, add the egg and water. Mix well.

On a lightly floured surface, knead the dough until smooth. Using a rolling pin, roll out to one-half inch thickness.

Using a dog bone-shaped cookie cutter or a knife, cut out the biscuits. Place on a ungreased, cookie sheet and bake 25–30 minutes or until lightly browned.

Remove to a wire rack to cool completely. Of course, beware of any of your dog's possible allergies to wheat, eggs, or dairy products.

Pyrrhos's Biscuits

1 package dry yeast
1 teaspoon sugar
¼ cup warm water
2 cups beef broth, at room temperature
¼ cup milk
½ cup honey
1 egg, beaten
¼ cup margarine
1 teaspoon salt
2½ cups all-purpose flour
1 cup cornmeal
1 cup wheat germ
2 cups cracked wheat
¾ cup wheat bran
¾ cup oatmeal
¾ cup cheddar cheese, grated
3 cups whole wheat flour

TOPPING:

1 cup beef broth
½ teaspoon garlic powder
3 tablespoons oil

In a small bowl, dissolve yeast and sugar in warm water.

In a large bowl, combine beef broth, milk, honey, egg, bacon grease or margarine, and salt. Add yeast-water mixture and mix well. Stir in flour, cornmeal, wheat germ, cracked wheat, wheat bran, oatmeal, and cheese. Add whole wheat flour, one-half cup at a time, mixing well after each addition.

Knead in the final amounts of flour by hand to make a stiff dough. Continue to knead 4–5 minutes.

Pat or roll to ½ inch thickness. Cut into bone shapes and place on a greased baking sheet. Cover lightly and let it rise for 30 minutes. Brush with topping. Bake on ungreased, cookie sheet for 10 to 12 minutes at 350 degrees or until golden brown in edges.

Elissa's Dog Biscuits

1 cup bran
1½ cups whole meal flour
½ cup olive oil, sunflower, or soya (olive oil is great for their coat)
½ cup sunflower seeds
1 cup oatmeal
1 egg
1 cup milk or water
1 teaspoon brewer's yeast
½ teaspoon salt or kelp
½ cup coconut
1 comfrey leaf, finely chopped (can add parsley, etc.)

Preheat the oven to 350 degrees.

Mix everything together and form balls with your hands.

Place on an ungreased, cookie tray and flatten with a fork. Bake slowly until hard, 40–45 minutes. (I double the recipe, and it makes heaps, about 2 trays).

Celosia's Dog Biscuits

1 cup whole wheat flour
2 tablespoons wheat germ
¼ cup bran flakes
¼ cup soy flour
1 tablespoon molasses
2 tablespoons oil or fat
1 tablespoon kelp or salt
1 teaspoon sage
½ teaspoon bone meal
⅓ cup milk or water

Preheat the oven to 350 degrees.

Mix all ingredients together. Knead and shape into crescents, rounds, or sticks for dogs. (This is good for cats too. For them, roll out and cut into narrow strips or ribbons.)

Bake 25–30 minutes until lightly toasted. Watch the narrow strips as they tend to get done sooner than the others. If the biscuits are not hard enough, leave them in the oven with the heat turned off for an hour to harden.

Glazed Biscuits

2 teaspoons beef bouillon granules
⅓ cup canola oil
1 cup boiling water
2 cups rolled oats
¾ cup cornmeal
½ cup milk
1 cup cheddar cheese, grated
1 egg, beaten
1 cup rye flour
2 cups white flour

TOPPING:

1 egg white, beaten

Preheat the oven to 325 degrees.

Add bouillon and oil to boiling water, then add oats. Let the mixture stand for a few minutes. Stir in the cornmeal, milk, cheese, and egg. Slowly stir in the flour mixture.

Knead on a lightly floured surface until the dough is smooth and no longer sticky. Roll out to about one-fourth inch thick and cut into bone shapes.

Place on a greased baking sheet. Brush topping on the biscuits. Bake 45 minutes or until lightly browned on the bottom. Turn off the oven and leave the biscuits in until cool.

Hunter's Favorite Dog Biscuits

1 package dry yeast
1 teaspoon sugar
1 cup warm chicken broth
2 tablespoons molasses
1¾–2 cups all-purpose flour
1½ cups whole wheat flour
1½ cups cracked wheat
½ cup cornmeal
½ cup nonfat dry milk powder
2 teaspoons garlic powder
2 teaspoons salt

GLAZE:

1 tablespoon milk
1 egg, beaten Preheat the oven to 300 degrees.

BISCUITS: Dissolve the yeast and sugar in ¼ cup of warm water, 110–115 degrees, let bubble. Stir in broth and molasses.

Add 1 cup only of the all-purpose flour, then add the whole wheat flour, cracked wheat, cornmeal, nonfat powdered milk, and garlic salt, and mix well.

On a floured surface, knead in the remaining flour. Roll out half dough at a time, keeping rest in container as to not dry out. Roll out to 3/8 inche thick. Cut in desired shapes. Place on an ungreased baking sheet.

GLAZE: Brush the tops with the beaten egg and milk mixture. Repeat with the remaining dough.

Bake 45 minutes. Turn the oven off and let dry overnight.

Yields 42 to 48.

Jake's Dog Biscuits

2½ cups whole wheat flour
½ cup nonfat powdered milk
½ teaspoon garlic powder
½ teaspoon salt
1 teaspoon brown sugar
6 tablespoons margarine or shortening
1 egg, beaten
3 tablespoons liver powder
½ cup ice water

Preheat the oven to 350 degrees.

In a large bowl, combine flour, powdered milk, garlic powder, salt, and sugar. Cut in the margarine.

Mix in the egg, then add liver powder. Add ice water until the mixture forms a ball. Pat out dough ½ inch thick on a lightly greased cookie sheet. Cut with any size cookie cutter. Remove scrapes and recut.

Bake 30 minutes.

Quick Peanut Butter and Honey Dog Biscuits

¾ cup all-purpose flour
1 egg
1 tablespoon honey
1 teaspoon peanut butter
¼ cup vegetable shortening
1 teaspoon baking soda
¼ teaspoon salt
¼ cup uncooked, rolled oats
½ teaspoon vanilla extract

Preheat the oven to 350 degrees.

Heat honey and peanut butter until runny (about 20 seconds in the microwave). Mix other ingredients together and drop by ½ teaspoonful onto an ungreased, cookie sheet.

Bake 8–10 minutes.

Yields 45 to 50 biscuits.

Peanut Butter Dog Biscuits

2½ cups whole wheat flour
½ cup nonfat milk powder
1½ teaspoons sugar
1 teaspoon salt
1 egg
8 ounces peanut butter (1 jar)
1 tablespoon garlic powder
½ cup cold water

Preheat the oven to 350 degrees.

Mix above ingredients together, adding water after other ingredients are mixed in. Knead 3–5 minutes. Dough should form a ball.

Roll to ½ inch thick and cut into doggie bone shapes.

Bake on a lightly greased cookie sheet 30 minutes.

Pumpkin-Patch Dog Biscuits

1½ cups whole wheat flour
1 tablespoon brown sugar
½ teaspoon ground cinnamon
½ teaspoon ground nutmeg
4 tablespoons butter-flavored Crisco
½ cup pumpkin, canned
1 egg
½ cup buttermilk

Preheat the oven to 400 degrees.

Combine flour, cinnamon, and nutmeg and cut in shortening. Beat egg with milk and pumpkin and combine with flour, mixing well. Stir until soft dough forms.

Drop by tablespoons onto an ungreased cookie sheet and bake 12–15 minutes.

Cool and serve.

Traildog Biscuits

1½ cups all-purpose flour
1½ cups whole wheat flour
1 teaspoon garlic powder
1 cup rye flour
1 egg, beaten
1 cup oats
½ cup vegetable oil
1 cup cornmeal
1¾ cups beef or chicken broth
¼ cup liver powder, available in health food stores

Preheat the oven to 300 degrees.

Mix all dry ingredients in a large bowl. Add egg, oil, and beef broth. Mix the dough, adding enough additional flour to make a dough that can be rolled.

On a floured surface, roll to ½ inch thickness, then cut into shapes or squares. Prick with a fork all over.

Bake 2 hours. Turn the oven off and let biscuits stand in the oven overnight to harden. Store in airtight containers.

Vegetarian Dog Biscuits

2½ cups all-purpose flour
¾ cup nonfat powdered milk
½ cup vegetable oil
2 tablespoons brown sugar
¾ cup vegetable broth
½ cup carrots, optional
1 egg

Preheat the oven to 300 degrees.

Mix all ingredients into a ball and roll out to about ¼ inch thick. Cut with bone-shaped cookie cutter or other cutter of your choice, or into strips.

Place on an ungreased cookie sheet and bake 30 minutes.

Veggie Bones

3 cups parsley, minced
¼ cup carrots, shredded
¼ cup mozzarella cheese, shredded
2 tablespoons olive oil
2¾ cups all-purpose flour
2 tablespoons bran
2 teaspoons baking powder
½ cup water (or more)

Preheat the oven to 350 degrees.

Stir together parsley, carrots, cheese, and oil. Combine all the dry ingredients and add to the veggies. Gradually add ½ cup of water, mixing well. Makes a moist but not wet dough. If needed, add a little more water. Knead 1 minute.

Roll out dough to ½ inch thickness. Using a cookie cutter, cut out the shapes and transfer them to a lightly greased baking sheet. Reroll the scraps and continue to cut the dough until it is all used up.

Bake 20–30 minutes in the middle of the oven until biscuits have browned and hardened slightly. They will harden more as they cool.

Store in an airtight container, at room temperature.

Western Ranch Biscuits

1 package dry yeast
1 teaspoon sugar
¼ cup warm water
2 cups beef broth, warm
¼ cup milk
½ cup honey
1 egg, beaten
¼ cup bacon grease or margarine
1 teaspoon salt
2½ cups flour (white, oat, or rye)
1 cup cornmeal
1 cup wheat germ
2 cups cracked wheat
¾ cup wheat bran
¾ cup oatmeal
¾ cup cheddar cheese, grated
3 cups whole wheat flour (approximately)

TOPPING:

1 cup beef broth
½ teaspoon garlic powder
3 tablespoons oil

Preheat the oven to 350 degrees.

In a small bowl, dissolve yeast and sugar in warm water, let bubble. In a large bowl, combine beef broth, milk, honey, egg, bacon grease or margarine, and salt. Add the yeast-water mixture and mix well.

Stir in flour, cornmeal, wheat germ, cracked wheat, wheat bran, oatmeal, and cheese.

Add whole wheat flour, one-half cup at a time, mixing well after each addition. Knead in the final amounts of flour by hand to make a stiff dough.

Continue to knead 4–5 minutes. Pat or roll to one-half inch thickness.

Cut into bone shapes and place on a greased baking sheet. Cover lightly and let rise for 30 minutes.

Bake 45 minutes or until lightly browned on the bottom.

Prepare topping during the last few minutes of baking. Turn off the oven heat. Remove biscuits from the oven. Immediately dip biscuits in the topping. Return them to the oven and leave biscuits in the oven for several hours or overnight.

Wheatless Tuna Biscuits

1 cup yellow cornmeal, *see Note
1 cup oatmeal
¼ teaspoon baking powder
½ teaspoon garlic powder
1 small can tuna in oil, undrained
⅓ cup water

Preheat the oven to 350 degrees.

Grind oatmeal in a processor to make a coarse flour. Set aside in a small bowl.

In the food processor, combine tuna with the oil and water, then add all the rest of the ingredients. Pulse till the mixture forms a ball. Then knead 2–3 minutes.

Knead on a floured surface till it forms a soft ball of dough. Roll out to a one-eighth–one-fourth inch thickness. Cut into shapes.

Bake on a lightly greased cookie sheet 20–25 minutes.

Cool completely.

*Note: or ¼ cup corn flour

Wholesome Whole Wheat Biscuits

2½ cups whole wheat flour
½ cup self-rising flour
1 tablespoon beef bouillon packet
3 tablespoons nonfat powdered milk, optional
2 cloves garlic, crushed
1 egg, beaten
1 tablespoon molasses
3 tablespoons canola oil
¼ cup water
2 tablespoons water

Preheat the oven to 300 degrees.

Measure dry ingredients into a bowl. Blend in all other ingredients and chill for 1 hour. Mix all together to form dough.

On a floured surface, roll dough to 1/8 inch thickness and cut with cookie cutters or into 1 x 3 inch strips.

Bake on ungreased, cookie sheets for 30 minutes. Brush with melted butter, before baking, if desired. Cool and serve.

Wolf-Dog Biscuits

2 cups whole wheat flour
¾ cup cornmeal
4 tablespoons vegetable oil
2 cups all-purpose flour
4 beef bouillon cubes
2 cups boiling water
10 tablespoons bacon bits

Preheat the oven to 300 degrees.

Combine first four ingredients; mix well. Dissolve bouillon cubes in boiling water and add bouillon to the flour mixture. Mix to make a stiff dough.

Roll onto a floured surface. Cut out shapes with cookie cutters (or a drinking glass turned upside down can be used). Bake 30 minutes. Turn oven off, let stand in oven overnight to harden.

Variations: Use clear gravies from turkey, roast beef, etc., in place of bouillon cubes. Crisp sausage bits could be used in place of bacon. Different spices could also be used (Italian, garlic, parsley, thyme, etc.).

Treats and Snacks

An Apple-a-Day Dog Treat

2 cups whole wheat flour
½ cup unbleached flour
½ cup cornmeal
1 apple, chopped or grated
1 egg, beaten
⅓ cup vegetable oil
1 tablespoon brown sugar, packed
⅜ cup water

Preheat the oven to 350 degrees.

Spray a cookie sheet with vegetable oil spray. Lightly dust your work surface with flour.

Blend flours and cornmeal in a large mixing bowl. Add apple, egg, oil, brown sugar, and water. Mix until well blended.

On a floured surface, roll dough out to ½ inch thickness.

Cut with cookie cutters of your desired shape and size.

Bake 35–40 minutes. Turn off the oven. Leave the door closed 1 hour to crisp treats. Remove treats from the oven.

Store baked treats in airtight containers or plastic bags and place in the refrigerator or freezer.

Yields 2 to 2½ dozen.

Alfalfa Hearts

2 cups whole wheat flour
½ cup soy flour
1 teaspoon bone meal, optional
2 tablespoons nutritional yeast
1 tablespoon lecithin, optional
½ teaspoon salt
¼ teaspoon garlic powder
3 tablespoons alfalfa sprouts, chopped
1 cup brown rice, cooked
3 tablespoons canola oil
½ cup water

Preheat the oven to 350 degrees.

Combine flours, bone meal, yeast, lecithin, salt, garlic powder, and alfalfa leaves. Add rice and oil. Mix well.

Add ¼ cup of water and mix. The dough should be very easy to handle, not crumbly. Add more water if needed to achieve the proper consistency.

Lightly flour the board or counter and roll out dough to ¼ inch thickness. Cut with a 2½ inch cookie cutter or use drinking glass as cutter.

Bake 25 minutes.

Yields 3 dozen.

Bacon Bites

    3 cups whole wheat flour
    ½ cup milk
    1 egg
    ¼ cup bacon grease or vegetable oil
    1 teaspoon garlic powder
    4 slices bacon, crumbled
    ½ cup cold water

Preheat the oven to 325 degrees.

Mix ingredients together thoroughly. Roll out on a floured surface to ¼ inch thickness. Place on ungreased, cookie sheet.

Bake 35–40 minutes.

Bacon Bits for Dogs

6 slices cooked bacon, crumbled
4 eggs, well beaten
⅛ cup bacon grease
1 cup water
½ cup nonfat powdered milk
2 cups graham flour
2 cups wheat germ
½ cup cornmeal

Preheat the oven to 350 degrees.

Mix all ingredients with a spoon. Drop by heaping tablespoonful onto a greased baking sheet.

Bake 15 minutes. Turn off the oven and leave cookies on the baking sheet in the oven overnight to dry out.

Beef and Rice Rounds

1 jar baby food, vegetables and beef
2½ cups flour, all-purpose
1 cup whole wheat flour
1 cup rice
1 package unflavored gelatin
1 egg
2 tablespoons vegetable oil
1 cup nonfat powdered milk
1 package yeast
1 teaspoon sugar
¼ cup warm water
1 beef bouillon cube

Preheat the oven to 300 degrees.

Dissolve yeast and sugar in warm water, let bubble. Mix dry ingredients in a large bowl. Add yeast, egg, oil, baby food, and dissolved beef bouillon.

Mix well. The mixture will be very dry. Knead with your hands until it forms a ball. Roll out on a floured surface to ¼ inch thick, then cut in 1 or 2 inch circles. (Can use drinking glass as cutter.)

Bake on an ungreased cookie sheet 30 minutes. Store in the refrigerator.

Beef Twisters

3½ cups flour, all-purpose
1 cup cornmeal
1 package unflavored gelatin
¼ cup milk
1 egg, beaten
¼ cup corn oil
1 jar (3½ ounces) baby food, meat
1 beef bouillon cube
¾ cup boiling water or beef stock

Preheat the oven to 400 degrees.

Dissolve the bouillon cube in water. Sift dry ingredients in a large bowl. Add milk, egg, oil, meat, and beef bouillon. Stir until well mixed.

Roll out onto a floured surface to ¼ inch thick. Cut in ¼ by 3 inch strips, twisting each strip 3 turns before placing on a cookie sheet.

Bake 35–40 minutes. Place in a container and refrigerate.

Banana Bites

2¼ cups whole wheat flour
½ cup nonfat powdered milk
1 egg
⅓ cup banana, ripe, mashed
¼ cup vegetable oil
1 beef bouillon cube
½ cup hot water
1 tablespoon brown sugar

Preheat the oven to 300 degrees.

Mix all ingredients until well blended. Knead for 2 minutes on a floured surface. Roll to ¼ inch thick. Use a bone-shaped cookie cutter or any one you prefer.

Bake 30 minutes on ungreased cookie sheets.

Carob Crunchies

2¼ cups whole wheat flour
1 egg
¼ cup applesauce
¼ cup vegetable oil
1 beef or chicken bouillon cube
½ cup hot water
1 tablespoon honey
1 tablespoon molasses
1 cup carob chips

Preheat the oven to 300 degrees.

Mix all ingredients except the carob chips together until well blended. Knead dough two minutes on a lightly floured surface. Roll to ¼ inch thickness.

Bake on an ungreased cookie sheet 30 minutes. Cool.

Melt carob chips in a microwave or saucepan. Dip cool biscuits in the melted carob liquid or lay on a flat surface and brush carob over the biscuits with a pastry brush. Let cool.

Cheese & Veggie Chews

½ cup cheddar cheese, grated, at room temperature
3 tablespoons vegetable oil
3 teaspoons applesauce
½ cup vegetables, any type
1 clove garlic, crushed
1 cup whole wheat flour
2 to 3 tablespoons nonfat powdered milk

Preheat the oven to 375 degrees.

Mix cheese, oil, and applesauce together. Add veggies, garlic, and flour. Combine thoroughly. Add just enough milk to help form a ball. Cover and chill for 1 hour.

Roll onto a floured surface and cut into shapes ¼ inch thick.

Bake 15 minutes or until golden brown. Cool.

Cheese 'N' Garlic Bites

1 cup wheat flour
1 cup cheddar cheese, grated
1 tablespoon garlic powder
1 tablespoon butter, softened
½ cup milk

Preheat the oven to 350 degrees.

Mix flour and cheese together. Add garlic powder and softened butter. Slowly add milk and form into a stiff dough. You may not need all of the milk.

Knead on a floured board for a few minutes. Roll out to ¼ inch thick. Cut into shapes and place on an ungreased cookie sheet.

Bake 15 minutes. Cool in the oven with the door slightly open until cold and firm. Refrigerate to keep fresh.

Chicken Liver Crisps

1 pound chicken liver
3 cups oatmeal (old-fashioned rolled oats, not instant or quick)

Preheat the oven to 350 degrees.

Put the chicken liver and the oatmeal in a food processor. Process until it is smooth and creamy. Line cookie sheet with parchment paper, then spread the paste out thinly on the cookie sheet using a spatula to about ¼ inch thick.

Bake 45 minutes. Remove from the oven and allow to cool until you can handle the parchment sheet. (Leave the oven on for now.)

Slide the parchment sheet off the cookie sheet onto a cutting board and cut into small squares (about ½ inch square is ideal) with a pizza cutter.

After you cut it into small squares, put it back on the cookie sheet and return it to the oven. Turn off the oven and leave the food in the oven overnight.

Store in a bag and freeze.

Delights

1 ripe banana
½ cup peanut butter
¼ cup wheat germ
¼ cup unsalted peanuts, chopped

In a small bowl, mash banana and peanut butter together using a fork. Mix in wheat germ. Place in the refrigerator for about an hour until firm.

With your hands, roll rounded teaspoonful of mixture into balls. Roll balls in peanuts, coating them evenly.

Place on a cookie sheet in the freezer. When completely frozen, pack into airtight containers and store in the freezer.

Dog Munchies

3 cups whole wheat flour
1 teaspoon garlic powder
½ cup bacon fat
1 cup cheddar cheese, shredded
1 egg, beaten slightly
1 cup milk

Preheat the oven to 400 degrees.

Place flour and garlic powder in a large bowl. Stir in bacon fat. Add cheese and egg. Gradually add enough milk to form a dough. Knead dough and roll out to about 1 inch thick, on floured surface.

Use dog-bone cookie cutters to cut out dough. Place on a greased cookie sheet.

Bake 12 minutes or until they start to brown. Cool and store in an airtight container.

Sarina's Favorite Treats

1 cup oatmeal
⅓ cup butter
1 teaspoon beef bouillon granules
½ cup hot water
¾ cup nonfat powdered milk
¾ cup cornmeal
1 egg, beaten
3 cups whole wheat flour

Preheat the oven to 325 degrees.

Combine oatmeal, butter, and bouillon granules in a large bowl. Pour hot water over this and let stand for 5 minutes.

Stir in powdered milk, cornmeal, and egg. Add flour ½ cup at a time, mixing well after each addition.

Knead 3–4 minutes, adding more flour if needed to make a very stiff dough. Roll out dough to ½ inch thickness, then cut into bone-shaped pieces.

Place on a greased cookie sheet.

Bake 50 minutes, then turn off the oven, and open the door slightly. Allow to cool and dry out overnight. Store in airtight container.

Good Gobblers

1 cup white flour
1 cup whole wheat flour
¼ cup sunflower seeds, chopped
2 tablespoons applesauce
1 tablespoon peanut butter
¼ cup molasses
2 eggs, beaten
¼ cup milk

Preheat the oven to 350 degrees.

Mix the dry ingredients together. Add applesauce, peanut butter, and molasses, and stir well.

In a separate bowl, mix the egg and milk together. Add to the dry mixture. Add a little more milk if the mixture is too dry. The dough should be firm. Knead for a few minutes. Roll out to ½ inch thickness, on floured surface. Cut into desired shapes. Place on ungreased, cookie sheet.

Bake 30 minutes or until biscuits are brown and firm.

Healthy Snacks

1 cup white rice flour
¼ cup soy flour
¼ cup egg substitute
1 tablespoon molasses
⅓ cup milk
⅓ cup nonfat powdered milk
2 tablespoons vegetable oil

Preheat the oven to 350 degrees.

Mix dry ingredients together. Add molasses, egg, oil, and milk. Roll out to ½ inch thick on a floured surface and cut into ½ inch pieces.

Bake 20 minutes on ungreased, cookie sheet.

Cool and store in tightly sealed containers.

Homemade Liver Treats

1 cup whole wheat flour
1 cup cornmeal
½ cup wheat germ
1 teaspoon garlic powder
1 pound beef liver

Preheat the oven to 350 degrees.

Liquefy liver in a blender, then add the dry ingredients. Grease a cookie sheet. Drop teaspoonful of mixture onto the cookie sheet and flatten with the bottom of a glass dipped in water and cornmeal.

Bake 15–20 minutes.

Store in airtight containers.

Dried Liver Treats

1 pound beef liver

Cut the liver into approximately 1/8 thick, 1 inch slices. Place in your food dehydrator for 24 hours. Spray the drying racks so the liver does not stick to the racks.

Liver Treats

1 pound beef liver
2 garlic cloves
1 box corn muffin mix

Preheat the oven according to the temperature on the corn muffin box.

Mix liver and garlic in a blender or food processor, then process till it liquefies. Stir in the muffin mix, then scrape onto a greased, baking sheet and pat to approximately a ½ inch thick.

Bake till very firm, but not burned.

Cut into squares and let cool. Store in the refrigerator or freezer.

Liver Slivers

½ pound chicken livers, cooked
1 cup chicken stock
½ cup corn oil
1 tablespoon parsley, chopped
1 cup nonfat powdered milk
1 cup rolled oats
½ cup brewer's yeast
1 cup soy flour
1 cup cornmeal
3 cups whole wheat flour

Preheat the oven to 350 degrees.

In a food processor or blender, process chicken livers, chicken stock, corn oil, and parsley until smooth.

Transfer to a large bowl. Add powdered milk, rolled oats, brewer's yeast, soy flour, and cornmeal. Mix well. Gradually add whole wheat flour. Knead with hands to mix in as much of the flour as it takes to create a very stiff dough.

Roll dough out to ¼ inch thick and cut into stick shapes, about ½ by 4 inches, on floured surface.

Bake on an ungreased cookie sheet 20–25 minutes until lightly browned and crisp. Turn off the heat and let biscuits dry out in the oven for several hours or overnight.

Place in containers and store in the refrigerator.

Crunchy Meat Treats

½ cup nonfat powdered milk
1 egg, beaten
1½ cups rice flour
½ teaspoon honey
½ cup water
5 teaspoons beef or chicken broth
1 jar baby food, beef, strained

Preheat the oven to 350 degrees.

Combine all ingredients well. Form into a ball. Roll dough out on a floured surface. Cut into desired shapes.

Bake 25–30 minutes.

Cool. The treats should be hard and crunchy.

Pet Party Mix

2 cups Cheerios
2 cups Chex mix
2 teaspoons dry brown gravy mix
½ cup bacon bits
2 cups Shredded Wheat, spoon size
½ cup melted butter or margarine
½ cup American cheese, grated
1 piece beef jerky (or Pupperoni, Jerky Treats, etc.)

Preheat the oven to 275 degrees.

Pour melted butter/margarine into a bowl. Stir in cheese, bacon bits, and gravy mix. Add cereal and stir until all pieces are coated.

Pour onto greased, cookie sheet and flatten out.

Bake until crisp, approximately 45 minutes.

Cool and store in a tightly sealed container.

Pet Puffs

1 package dry yeast
1 teaspoon sugar
¼ cup warm water (110–115 F)
1½ cups whole wheat flour
1 cup all-purpose flour
1 package unflavored gelatin
1 cup nonfat dry milk powder
¼ cup corn oil
1 egg
1 can dog food (6–8 ounces)
¼ cup water

Preheat the oven to 300 degrees.

Dissolve yeast and sugar in the warm water, let bubble. Mix dry ingredients. Add all ingredients together. (The dough will be very stiff; it may be necessary to mix it with your hands.)

Drop dough by level teaspoons onto an ungreased cookie sheet.

Bake 25 minutes.

Peanut Butter Swirls

DOUGH #1

4 cups whole wheat flour
½ cup cornmeal
1⅓ cups water
⅓ cup peanut butter
1 egg

DOUGH #2

4 cups whole wheat flour
⅔ cup cornmeal
½ cup banana, mashed
1 egg
1¼ cups water
2 tablespoons vegetable oil
2 tablespoons molasses
2 tablespoons cinnamon

Combine all #1 ingredients and mix thoroughly. Knead on a lightly floured surface. Set aside.

Combine all #2 ingredients and mix thoroughly. Knead on a lightly floured surface.

Roll each dough mixture separately to a 1/8 inch thickness, then cut into 1 by 3 inch rectangles. Lightly brush a little water over the top of the light dough. Place the dark dough on top of light dough, then roll up like a jelly roll. Wrap the roll in plastic and chill in the freezer for 1 hour. Cut the roll into ¼ inch slices. Place them on a cookie sheet sprayed with nonstick spray.

Bake 1 hour at 350 degrees.

Carrot Treats

½ cup cheddar cheese, shredded
¼ cup margarine (½ half stick)
1 drop red food coloring or more if needed
1 drop yellow food coloring or more if needed
1 jar baby food, carrots
1 cup all-purpose flour
½ teaspoon garlic powder
¼ cup milk or more if needed

Preheat the oven to 350 degrees.

Melt cheese and margarine in a saucepan, stirring frequently. Remove from the heat. Stir in food dye to make an orange color. Add carrots, flour, and garlic powder. Stir until well blended. Add enough milk to form into a ball.

Transfer to a mixing bowl and chill for 1 hour.

Roll the dough on a lightly floured, flat surface to ¼ inch thick. Place on a cookie sheet lightly sprayed with nonstick cooking spray.

Bake 20–30 minutes or until golden brown. Cool completely

Puppy Pretzels

1 teaspoon brown sugar
2 teaspoons dry yeast
1 teaspoon sugar
⅔ cup water
¾ cup whole wheat flour
3 tablespoons soy flour, low fat
¼ cup nonfat powdered milk
1 tablespoon dried liver powder
1 tablespoon bone meal flour
¾ teaspoon salt
1 egg, beaten (½ in recipe, ½ in glaze)
2 tablespoons cooking oil
3 tablespoons wheat germ

Preheat the oven to 375 degrees.

Dissolve yeast and sugar in warm water, let bubble.

Combine all the dry ingredients. Add half of the beaten egg, and the oil, and yeast-water mixture. Mix well.

Knead on a floured surface until the dough is firm. Place in an oiled bowl, cover, and let rise until double in size.

Shape into pretzels and place on a greased cookie sheet.

Bake 15 minutes.

Remove and brush with the remaining beaten egg and sprinkle with wheat germ. Return to the oven and bake at 300 degrees for 15 minutes until nicely browned and quite firm.

Note: You may omit liver powder and bone meal flour if you have difficulty locating them.

Cayenne's Rewards

1 package dry yeast
1 teaspoon sugar
2 cups all-purpose flour
2 cups whole wheat flour
2 cups cornmeal
2 cups oatmeal, uncooked
1 cup fresh mint leaves, chopped, loosely packed
1 cup parsley sprigs, chopped, loosely packed
½ cup toasted wheat germ
1 can beef broth (13¾–14½ ounces)
¾ cup milk

Preheat the oven to 350 degrees.

In a small bowl, combine yeast, sugar, and ¼ cup of warm water (105 degrees to 115 degrees F.). Let stand until yeast foams, about 5 minutes.

In a very large bowl, combine all-purpose flour, whole wheat flour, cornmeal, oats, mint, parsley, and wheat germ. With a wooden spoon, stir in yeast mixture, broth, and milk until combined. With hands, knead dough in the bowl until blended, about 1 minute.

Divide dough in half. Cover 1 piece with plastic wrap to prevent drying out. Place the remaining piece of dough on a lightly floured surface. With a floured rolling pin, roll dough to ¼ inch thick. Cut with cookie cutters, then reroll the trimmings and cut more biscuits with the remaining dough.

With a spatula, transfer biscuits to a large ungreased cookie sheet.

Bake small biscuits 30 minutes, bake large biscuits 40 minutes. Turn the oven off and leave the biscuits in the oven 1 hour to dry out.

Remove the biscuits from the cookie sheet and place on a wire rack to cool. Store at room temperature in tightly sealed containers.

Yields about 4 dozen large biscuits or 8 dozen small biscuits.

Salmon Treats

1 can salmon, pink
½ cup chopped parsley
3 eggs, shells included
½ cup sesame seeds, ground in coffee grinder
½ cup flaxseeds, ground in coffee grinder
2–3 cups potato flour

Preheat the oven to 375 degrees.

Put all ingredients except the potato flour into a food processor and mix VERY WELL. Pour potato flour through the opening while the motor is running. Add enough so the dough forms, like a pie crust, and rolls into a ball. It is then ready to take out.

Dump the dough onto a potato floured counter. Knead for a few minutes and roll out into a ¼ inch thick. Cut into small squares.

Bake on cookie sheets, lightly sprayed with nonstick cooking spray or line the sheet with parchment paper.

Bake 30 minutes.

Snicker-Poodles

½ cup vegetable oil
½ cup shortening
1 cup honey
2 eggs
3¾ cups white flour
2 teaspoons cream of tartar
1 teaspoon baking soda
½ cup cornmeal
2 teaspoons cinnamon

Preheat the oven to 400 degrees.

Mix vegetable oil, shortening, and honey together until smooth. Add eggs and beat well. Blend in flour, baking soda, and cream of tartar. Knead dough until mixed well.

Shape the dough by rounded teaspoon into balls. Mix the cornmeal and cinnamon together in a bowl and roll balls in the mixture. Place 2 inches apart on a cookie sheet that has been sprayed with a nonstick spray. Press the balls down with a fork.

Bake 8 minutes. Remove from the cookie sheet and cool on a rack.

Sunrise Snacks

¼ cup hot water
8 chicken or beef bouillon cubes
1 teaspoon sugar
1 package dry yeast
1½ cups tomato juice
2 cups all-purpose flour, divided
2 cups wheat germ
1½ cups whole wheat flour

Preheat the oven to 325 degrees.

Place the hot water, sugar, and bouillon cubes in a large mixing bowl and mash with a fork. Sprinkle yeast over this mixture and let stand about 5 minutes, until yeast is dissolved and foams. Add the tomato juice, half the flour, and the wheat germ, and stir to form a smooth batter.

Gradually work in the remaining flour and the whole wheat flour with your hands. Divide the dough into 4 balls. Roll each ball out on a floured board to about ¼ inch thick. Cut into shapes and place on ungreased cookie sheets about an inch apart.

Bake 1 hour, then turn off the heat and let biscuits dry in the oven for about 4 hours or overnight with the door propped open slightly.

Store in airtight containers.

Training Treats

2⅓ cups flour, all-purpose or whole wheat
¼ cup olive oil
¼ cup applesauce
½ cup Parmesan cheese, grated
1 large egg
1 teaspoon garlic powder
¼ cup nonfat powdered milk

Preheat the oven to 350 degrees.

Combine all ingredients in a large bowl and mix well. Roll the dough out to the size of a cookie sheet, about ¼ inch think. Pat the dough onto a lightly greased cookie sheet, bringing it to the edges. Using a sharp knife or a pizza cutter, cut to ½ inch squares. If you're using these as training treats, cut them into smaller pieces. Sprinkle a little extra cheese, if desired, on the dough for flavor.

Bake 15 minutes or until golden brown. Turn off the oven and let cool for a few hours in the oven.

Store in airtight containers or in the freezer.

Tasty Treats

1 cup oatmeal, quick
¼ cup margarine
1½ cups hot water
½ cup nonfat powdered milk
1 cup Cheddar, Swiss, or Colby cheese, grated
¼ teaspoon garlic powder
1 egg, beaten
1 cup cornmeal
1 cup wheat germ
3 cups whole wheat flour
1 tablespoon beef or chicken bouillon

Preheat the oven to 300 degrees.

In a large bowl, pour hot water over the oatmeal and margarine, then cut into small pieces and let stand 5 minutes.

Stir in powdered milk, grated cheese, garlic powder, bouillon, and the egg. Add cornmeal and wheat germ. Mix well.

Add flour, ½ cup at a time, mixing well after each addition. Knead 3 to 4 minutes, adding more flour if necessary to make a very stiff dough.

Roll dough to ½ inch thickness. Cut into bone-shaped biscuits and place on a greased cookie sheet.

Bake 1 hour. Turn off the heat and leave in the oven an additional 2–4 hours.

Yields approximately 2¼ pounds.

Turkey Treats

2 cups cooked turkey, cut up
2 cloves garlic
4 teaspoons cheddar cheese, grated
1 tablespoon parsley, freshly chopped
2 eggs
2 cups whole wheat flour
2 tablespoons brewer's yeast
2 tablespoons vegetable oil

Preheat the oven to 350 degrees.

Combine turkey, garlic, cheese, parsley, and mix well. Beat the eggs in a bowl and pour over the turkey mixture. Add the flour, yeast, and oil. Stir until thoroughly mixed and all ingredients are coated. Drop small lumps onto an ungreased cookie sheet.

Bake 20 minutes, until brown and firm.

Store in refrigerator.

Wheat Treats

2 jars baby food, meat, strained
½ cup nonfat powdered milk
2 tablespoons wheat germ
⅓ cup water
½ cup all-purpose flour
1 teaspoon garlic powder

Preheat the oven to 325 degrees.

Mix all ingredients together. Roll out dough on a floured surface to ¼ inch think. Cut out with cookie cutters and place on a lightly greased cookie sheet.

Bake 30–35 minutes or until golden brown.

Popsicles and Cold Treats

Frozen Paw Treats

2 32 ounce tubs plain or vanilla yogurt
1 8 ounce can tuna in water
2 teaspoons garlic power
1 banana, apple, or can of crushed pineapple
24 3 ounce plastic Dixie cups

Mix all ingredients in a large bowl. Use a spoon and scoop the mixture into the Dixie cups. Place on a tray and freeze.

Yields approximately 24.

Frozen Puppy Paws

1 32 ounce tub plain or vanilla yogurt
2 tablespoons peanut butter
1 teaspoon garlic power
1 banana, apple, or can of crushed pineapple
12 3 ounce plastic Dixie cups

Mix all ingredients in a large bowl. Use a spoon and scoop the mixture into the Dixie cups. Place on a tray and freeze.

Yields approximately 24.

Peanut Butter Pupcicles

1 ripe banana
½ cup peanut butter
¼ cup wheat germ
¼ cup chopped peanuts

Mash the banana and peanut butter together, then stir in the wheat germ. Chill 1 hour. Place in containers, then store in your refrigerator or freezer.

Yogurt Pups

16 ounces plain nonfat yogurt
¾ cup water
1 tablespoon chicken bouillon granules

Dissolve bouillon in water, Combine water and yogurt in a blender and blend thoroughly. Pour into small containers for freezing, then cover and freeze.

PBJ Pops

2 cups plain yogurt, low-fat or fat-free
1 ripe banana
1 cup blueberries
3 tablespoons peanut butter, natural and salt-free is preferred
1 teaspoon vanilla extract

Stir all of the ingredients together in a medium bowl. Pour into a blender and purée until smooth.

Pour the smoothie into ice cube trays and freeze. They will last for 6 months or more in the freezer.

Yields 32 ice-cube dog treats.

Carob Chip

2 6 ounce containers plain yogurt (low-fat or fat-free)
1 tablespoon honey
⅓ cup carob chips

Mix all ingredients in a medium bowl until well combined. Spoon into an ice-cube tray or cupcake liners. Freeze until solid (it will take several hours).

Peanut Butter & Carob Swirl

1 32 ounce plain yogurt (low-fat or fat-free)
1 cup natural peanut butter
½ cup carob chips

Divide yogurt evenly into a 6 muffin cup pan with liners.

Pour peanut butter into a small bowl. Melt carob chips gradually in a microwave-safe bowl in the microwave. Stir after every 15 to 30 seconds. Pour the melted carob into the peanut butter. Stir until combined.

Place a spoonful of the peanut butter mixture on top of each muffin cup. Gently swirl the peanut butter mixture into the yogurt with a stick, just to swirl not mixed completely. Freeze until solid.

Chicken & Beef Broth Ice Cream for Dogs

½ cup water
½ cup beef
½ chicken broth

For your basic broth ice cubes, mix the water and broth, then pour into an ice cube tray and freeze.

For variety: **add a small meat, veggies, berries, dog treats, or dog food pieces into the ice-cube liquid before freezing.**

Pumpkin Pops

1 instant vanilla pudding mix
1 15 ounce can pumpkin purée (**not** pumpkin pie filling)
1 tablespoon pumpkin pie spice

Whisk the vanilla pudding mix, pumpkin pie spice, and milk together until dissolved, approximately 2 minutes. Fold, or gently stir in the pumpkin purée. Scoop pumpkin pudding into small paper cups and place in the freezer.

Miscellaneous Dog Stuff

Weight-On Meatballs

1½ pounds fatty raw hamburger
½ cup wheat germ oil or wheat germ
2 eggs
3 cups oatmeal
½ cup peanut butter
¼ cup molasses
¼ cup canola oil

Mix all ingredients together and form into meatballs. Place the meatballs on a cookie sheet or glass baking dish and put in the freezer. Once they are frozen, put them in another container. Give 2 to 3 meatballs per day to your pet depending on your dog's size, with their regular food. Microwave the meatballs about 30 seconds before serving. These are also good for the fussy or picky eater!

Dog Oil Supplement

¼ cup olive oil
¼ cup canola oil
¼ cup cod liver oil
¼ cup flaxseed oil

Place all the oils in a brown bottle and shake well. Store in the refrigerator.

Add 2 teaspoons to the dog's food each day. Can be added to dry food as well.

Safflower and sunflower oil may also be used. Helps to promote a healthy coat.

Dog Powder Mix

1 cup brewer's yeast
1 cup bone meal
½ cup kelp powder
½ cup alfalfa powder

Mix well and place in airtight containers. Keep in the freezer if desired. Add 1 tablespoon to your dog's food each day.

Doggie Dip

3 tablespoons peanut butter
2 tablespoons honey
1 jar banana baby food
1 16 ounce vanilla yogurt
1 tablespoon whole wheat flour

Mix the peanut butter, honey, and banana together until well blended.

In a separate bowl, combine the yogurt and flour; mix well.

Add the fruit mixture to the yogurt and blend together. Refrigerate.

Use this dip with biscuits and other treats. Allow treats to chill in the refrigerator until the coating is set and firm.

These are recipes that we have collected over the years while training and breeding our dogs. We have enjoyed making these for our dogs and thought it would be nice to have a cookbook collection of recipes for your furry family member, all in one place.

Enjoy!

CPSIA information can be obtained
at www.ICGtesting.com
Printed in the USA
BVOW08s1101291017
498948BV00002B/136/P